Great Appliqué:
Wonderful Small Quilts

Great Appliqué:
Wonderful Small Quilts

BETTER HOMES AND GARDENS® BOOKS

DES MOINES, IOWA

Better Homes and Gardens® Books, an imprint of Meredith® Books:
President, Book Group: Joseph J. Ward
Vice President, Editorial Director: Elizabeth P. Rice

Executive Editor: Maryanne Bannon
Senior Editor: Carol Spier
Selections Editor: Eleanor Levie
Technical Editor: Cyndi Marsico
Technical Assistant: Diane Rode Schneck
Copy Editor: Mary Butler
Book Design: Beth Tondreau Design
Technical Artist: Phoebe Adams Gaughan
Photographer: Steven Mays
Photo Stylist: Susan Piatt
Production Manager: Bill Rose

The editors would like to thank the Village of Waterloo museum,
Stanhope, New Jersey, and The Inn at Millrace Pond, Hope, New Jersey,
for sharing their premises for photography. Thanks also to James and Judith Milne
Antiques, and Susan Parrish Antiques, both in New York City, for their kind
assistance in the search for quilts to include in this volume.

ISBN: 0-696-00082-2
Library of Congress Catalog Card Number: 93-080854

Printed in the United States of America
10 9 8 7 6 5 4 3 2 1

All of us at Better Homes and Gardens® Books are dedicated to offering you,
our customer, the best books we can create. We are particularly concerned that all
of our instructions for making projects are clear and accurate.
Please address your correspondence to Customer Service, Meredith® Press,
150 East 52nd Street, New York, NY 10022.

If you would like to order additional copies of any of our books,
call 1-800-678-2803 or check with your local bookstore.

Contents

Quiltmaking offers wonderful variety. Using layered shapes of appliqué, the quiltmaker has freedom to create images that would be difficult to achieve with geometric piecing of patchwork. No more difficult than patchwork, appliqué is simply different. Many people find it less routine, more relaxing, forgiving and creative. The patterns here are for eight small quilts that you can re-create as shown or customize by using the **CHANGING COLORS** *feature that accompanies each. If appliqué is new to you, begin with the Flower and Bud Quilt, or make one block from the Country Folk Animals Quilt. Whatever your skill and enthusiasm, choose the design that most appeals to you—just bear in mind that the more pieces there are, the more time you will spend on your appliqué quilt. Enjoy!*

These symbols, found on the opening page of each project, identify suggested levels of experience needed to make the projects in this book. However, you will see within these pages many interpretations of each project, and the editors hope you will find for each something easily achievable or challenging, as you wish.

 New Quilter   *Confident Quilter*   *Expert Quilter*

Wreath of Flowers Quilt

BY MIMI SHIMMIN

I f at first glance you think that this little quilt is a traditional Baltimore Album block and then look again, only to decide it must be derived from an Eastern European folk design, you will be right—for when we asked Mimi Shimmin to design a Baltimore-style floral, we knew she would give it a folkloric spin. Although there are quite a few tiny pieces, if you fuse and then machine-stitch them to the background, you'll find this quilt fairly quick to make.

Note: All dimensions except for binding are finished size.

BLOCK
One block 17½″ square,
with appliqués

BINDING
2″-wide strip, pieced as necessary
and cut to size

GREAT APPLIQUÉ LAYOUT TIP

Instead of marking the guidelines for a complex design onto your background fabric, trace them onto a piece of clear acetate or heavy tracing paper. Center the tracing over your block, then slide the appliqués, one at a time, into position underneath it, pinning each in place. Or—tape the tracing onto a light box or window pane. Tape fabric over tracing. Pin appliqués in place.

*Note: All dimensions include ¼″ seam allowance
unless otherwise stated.*

Yardages are based on 44″ fabric. Use actual-size patterns on pages 80 to 81 to prepare templates #1 through #21 for machine-appliqué; see also *Appliqué Tips*, page 76, and *Machine-Appliqué*, page 78. Cut appliqués following chart; see *Using the Cutting Charts*, pages 74 to 75. Cut binding as directed below.

DIMENSIONS

FINISHED BLOCK
17½″ square; about 24¾″ diagonal

FINISHED QUILT
19″ square

GREAT FABRIC TIP

This little quilt is a wonderful scrap project. 1/4 yard quantities are listed since that is often the smallest cut a store will make, but you may find all the fabric you need in your scrap collection.

MATERIALS

WHITE SOLID
¾ yd.

YELLOW SOLID
¼ yd.

LT. MUSTARD FLORAL
¼ yd.

DK. MUSTARD FLORAL
¼ yd.

ORANGE FLORAL
¼ yd.

PINK SOLID
¼ yd.

RED SOLID
½ yd.

RED FLORAL
¼ yd.

BURGUNDY FLORAL
¼ yd.

LT. BLUE FLORAL
¼ yd.

ROYAL BLUE SOLID
¼ yd.

DK. BLUE SOLID
¼ yd.

MED. GREEN SOLID
¼ yd.

MED. GREEN FLORAL
¼ yd.

DK. GREEN SOLID
¼ yd.

DK. GREEN FLORAL
¼ yd.

BINDING
Use ½ yd. red solid to make a 2″ × 90″ strip (includes extra length). Reserve remainder of fabric for cutting appliqués #16 and #18.

BACKING *
¾ yd.

BATTING *

THREAD

*Backing and batting should be cut and pieced as necessary so they are at least 4″ larger on all sides than the quilt top, then trimmed to size after quilting.

Fabric and Yardage	Number of Pieces	Size/Shape
BLOCK		
White Solid ¾ yd.	1	19″ square
APPLIQUÉS		
Yellow Solid ¼ yd.	12	#2
	4	#5
	4	#12
	4	#21
Lt. Mustard Floral ¼ yd.	2	#4
Dk. Mustard Floral ¼ yd.	2	#4
Orange Floral ¼ yd.	2	#17

Fabric and Yardage	Number of Pieces	Size/Shape
APPLIQUÉS		
Pink Solid ¼ yd.	2	#7
	2	#7$_R$
Red Solid[1] ¼ yd.	2	#16
	4	#18
Red Floral ¼ yd.	4	#6
	2	#10
	4	#18
	4	#19
Burgundy Floral ¼ yd.	2	#11
	2	#13
	4	#18
	4	#20
Lt. Blue Floral ¼ yd.	4	#1
Royal Blue Solid ¼ yd.	4	#1

Fabric and Yardage	Number of Pieces	Size/Shape
APPLIQUÉS		
Dk. Blue Solid ¼ yd.	4	#1
Med. Green Solid ¼ yd.	22	#3
	2	#8
	2	#8$_R$
	2	#14
Med. Green Floral ¼ yd.	20	#3
	2	#9
	2	#9$_R$
Dk. Green Solid ¼ yd.	28	#3
Dk. Green Floral ¼ yd.	28	#3
	6	#15

[1] Use remainder of fabric from binding.
Note: Subscript R indicates reversed shape.

APPLIQUÉ

1. Mark guidelines for wreath placement on quilt block.
- Mark horizontal and vertical center lines completely across block.
- Align long dash lines on wreath half-pattern with center lines on block; transfer half-wreath.
- Rotate pattern 180° and realign guidelines, lapping ends of wreath halves symmetrically.

2. Mark guidelines for border placement on quilt block.
- Mark a 17″ square (¼″ inside seam line).
- Mark outlines of border flower in each corner, barely touching guidelines.
- Mark three berries at center of each side.

3. Prepare fabric shapes for machine-appliqué (see "Machine-Appliqué, page 78).

4. Arrange and secure all appliqués on block, aligning outlines of fabric shapes and guidelines, and lapping flowers over small leaves and stems as shown or as desired.

◆ *For border*: Make each leafy border segment by arranging 9 small leaves (#3) between each corner flower and center cluster of berries.

5. Machine-appliqué all shapes in place.

Finishing

1. Prepare batting and backing.

2. Assemble layers for quilting.

3. Quilt around inner and outer edges of wreath, ¼″ from appliqués, making two continuous lines of stitching.

4. Trim batting and backing to ¾″ beyond block seam line.

5. Bind quilt edges.

The palette Mimi Shimmin chose for her Wreath of Flowers may seem perfect, but it is hardly the only one that could lend charm to this design. Try other typical folkloric palettes, substitute pastels, or choose a dark background.

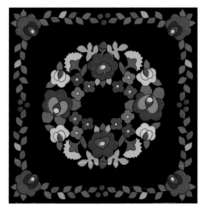

Photocopy this page, then create your own color scheme using colored pencils or markers. Refer to the examples shown, or design a unique color scheme to match your decor or please your fancy.

Country Folk Animals Quilt

BY KATHARINE BRAINARD

Katharine Brainard likes the clean silhouettes of folk art weathervanes and decided to capture them in this quilt, which was commissioned by a friend who was moving into a country home. Shapes suggestive of curvy waves, choppy grass, or shallow mounds ground the animals and keep them from floating on the blocks. Katharine does almost all of her appliqué and quilting by machine. Sashing with corner blocks is typical of her designs.

Note: All dimensions except for binding are finished size.

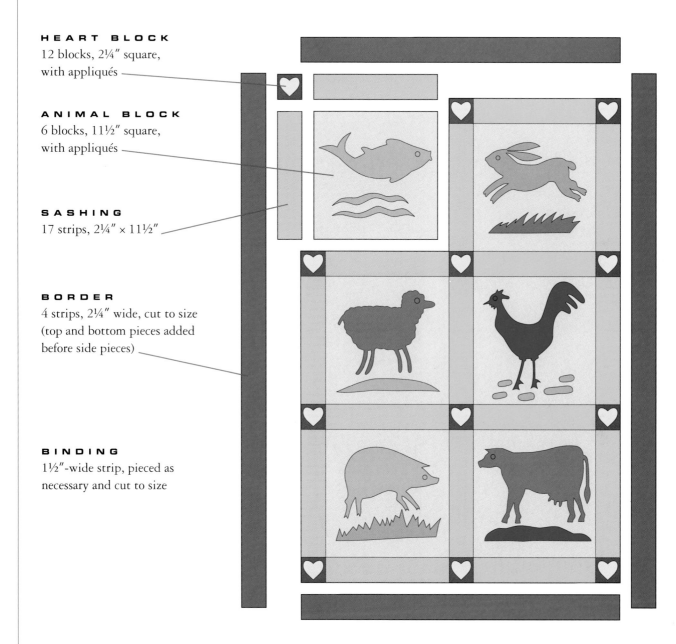

HEART BLOCK
12 blocks, 2¼″ square, with appliqués

ANIMAL BLOCK
6 blocks, 11½″ square, with appliqués

SASHING
17 strips, 2¼″ × 11½″

BORDER
4 strips, 2¼″ wide, cut to size (top and bottom pieces added before side pieces)

BINDING
1½″-wide strip, pieced as necessary and cut to size

*Note: All dimensions include ¼" seam allowance
unless otherwise stated.*

Yardages are based on 44" fabric. Enlarge and/or complete patterns on page 82, then prepare templates for machine-appliqué; see also *Appliqué Tips*, page 76, and *Hand-Appliqué*, page 77. Cut blocks, strips, and appliqués following charts; see *Using the Cutting Charts*, pages 74 to 75. Cut binding as directed below. Strips include extra length, unless otherwise stated.

DIMENSIONS

FINISHED ANIMAL BLOCK
11½" square; about 16¼" diagonal

FINISHED HEART BLOCK
2¼" square; about 3³⁄₁₆" diagonal

FINISHED QUILT
34¼" × 48"

MATERIALS

MUSLIN PRINT
¾ yd.

PINK STRIPE
¼ yd.

PINK PRINT
¾ yd.

BLUE CHECK
¼ yd.

BLUE ARGYLE
¼ yd.

BLUE FLORAL
¼ yd.

BLUE STRIPE
½ yd.

BLUE/PINK PRINT
1½ yds.

NAVY PRINT
¼ yd.

BINDING
¼ yd. contrasting pink print, cut and pieced to make a 1½" × 190" strip.

BACKING *
1½ yds.

BATTING *

THREAD

BUTTONS
6 clear, round buttons, ⅜" diameter

*Backing and batting should be cut and pieced as necessary so they are at least 4" larger on all sides than the quilt top, then trimmed to size after quilting.

GREAT SAFETY TIP

If you plan to give this or any other quilt to a small child, omit trims that could be swallowed, such as buttons or beads, replacing them with felt or embroidery.

FIRST CUT			SECOND CUT	
Fabric and Yardage	Number of Pieces	Size	Number of Pieces	Size
BLOCKS				
Muslin Print ¾ yd.	2	12" × 40"	6	12" square
Navy Print ¼ yd.	1	2¾" × 40"	12	2¾" square
SASHING				
Pink Print ¾ yd.	6	2¾" × 40"	17	2¾" × 12" (exact length)
BORDER				
Blue/Pink Print 1½ yds.	2	2¾" × 38"		
	2	2¾" × 52"		

	APPLIQUÉS		
	Number of Pieces		
Fabric and Yardage	For 6 Animal Blocks	For 12 Heart Blocks	Shape
Blue Check ¼ yd.	1	–	Fish
	1	–	Pig
	1	–	Upper Fish Wave
	1	–	Lower Fish Wave
	1	–	Sheep Grass
	1	–	Rooster Stones
Blue Argyle ¼ yd.	1	–	Bunny
	1	–	Pig Grass
Blue Floral ¼ yd.	1	–	Sheep
	1	–	Cow
	1	–	Bunny Grass
Blue Stripe ½ yd.	1	–	Rooster
	1	–	Cow Grass
Pink Stripe ¼ yd.	–	12	Heart

1. Prepare fabric shapes for machine-appliqué; see *Machine-Appliqué*, page 78.

2. Arrange and secure all appliqués on each block.

◆ *For Animal block:* Center overall design on block.

◆ *For Heart block:* Center heart on block.

3. Machine appliqué all shapes in place.

Sashing

Arrange units as shown. Join units to form 7 rows. Join rows.

Border

Join border to quilt center, shorter strips at top and bottom,
then longer strips at sides.

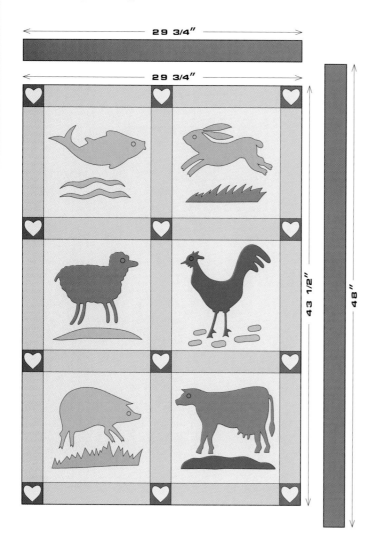

Finishing

1. Sew a button eye on each animal where indicated by the circle.

2. Prepare batting and backing.

3. Assemble layers for quilting.

4. Quilt in-the-ditch on all seams and around appliqués.
Quilt three parallel lines along the length of each sashing strip $9/16''$
from seams and from each other.

5. Trim batting and backing to $1/2''$ beyond block seam line.

6. Bind quilt edges.

You might try this quilt in black (or rusty gray) and white to really capture the look of the weathervanes that inspired it, or make it truly patriotic in red-white-and-blue. See what happens if you make the background dark or make each block in a different, but related, color scheme.

Photocopy this page, then create your own color scheme using colored pencils or markers. Refer to the examples shown, or design a unique color scheme to match your decor or please your fancy. Note how a single block, framed by sashing and corner blocks, would make a charming pillow.

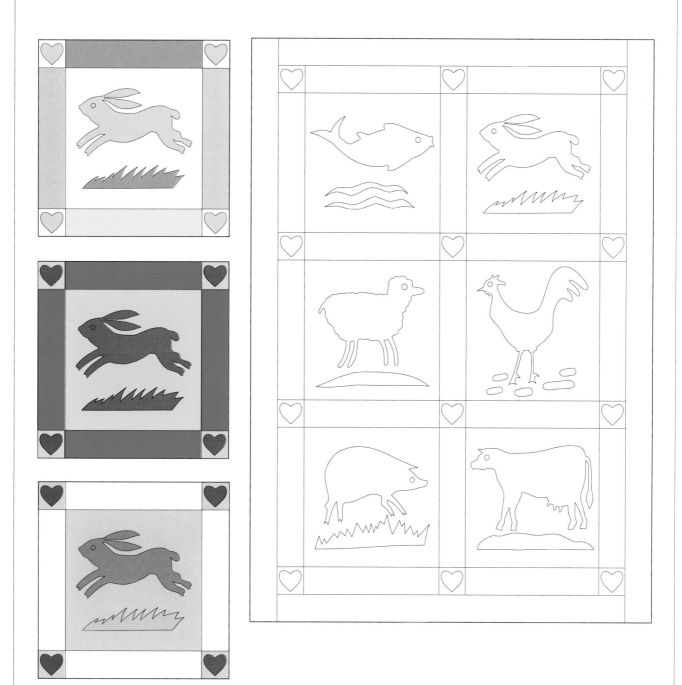

Noah's Ark Quilt

BY KINDRED SPIRITS:
SALLY KORTE AND ALICE STREBEL

Kindred Spirits is an Ohio-based pattern company noted for its primitive and funky designs that often feature dark-colored homespun plaids and stripes, less-than-perfect hand-stitchery, and button embellishments. This casual piece, made from cotton and wool fabrics, has lots of unfinished edges and a whimsical slashed-and-tied border. Appliqué is done with easy blanket or running stitches, but you could fuse most of the pieces together if you prefer.

Note: All dimensions are finished size.

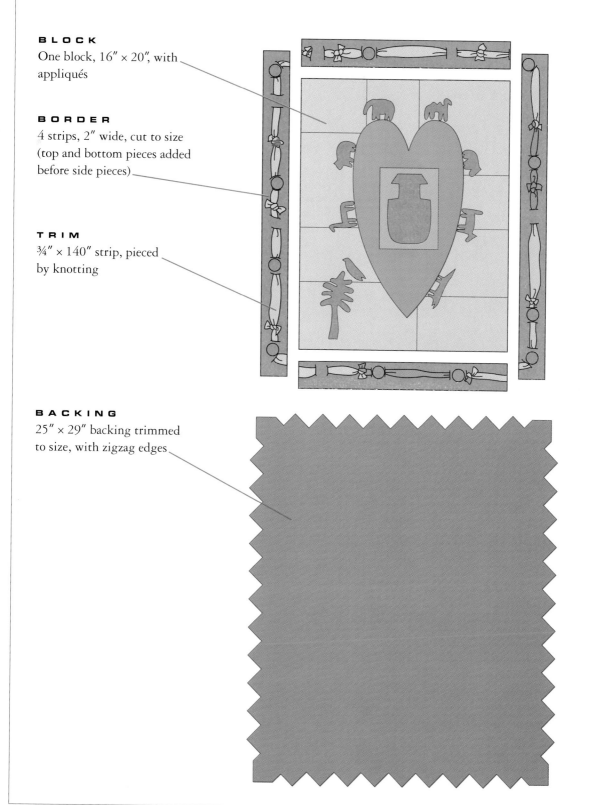

BLOCK

One block, 16″ × 20″, with appliqués

BORDER

4 strips, 2″ wide, cut to size (top and bottom pieces added before side pieces)

TRIM

¾″ × 140″ strip, pieced by knotting

BACKING

25″ × 29″ backing trimmed to size, with zigzag edges

Note: All dimensions include ¼" seam allowance unless otherwise stated.

Yardages are based on 44" fabric. Enlarge heart pattern on page 84, then use it and actual-size patterns on same page to prepare templates for hand-appliqué; see also *Appliqué Tips*, page 76, and *Hand-Appliqué*, page 77. Cut patches, strips, and appliqués following cutting schematics (which include seam allowance) and charts; see *Using the Cutting Charts*, pages 74 to 75. Cut border trim as directed below. Strips include extra length, unless otherwise stated.

DIMENSIONS

FINISHED BLOCK
16" × 20"

FINISHED QUILT
23" × 27"

MATERIALS

ASSORTED TAN PLAIDS AND STRIPES
½ yd.

BROWN PLAID
¼ yd.

RED PLAID
½ yd.

BLACK FELT OR MELTON CLOTH
½ yd.

BROWN FELT OR MELTON CLOTH
¾ yd. for backing

BORDER TRIM
Use remainder of fabric from patches to cut enough ¾"-wide strips to make a 140"-long strip. Do not join the cut strips until directed.

BATTING

THREAD

EMBROIDERY FLOSS
One skein each brown and black

BUTTONS
10 assorted round, brown buttons, ¾" diameter

CUTTING SCHEMATICS
(Seam allowance included)

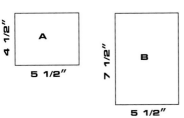

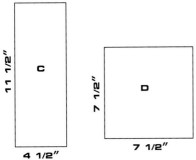

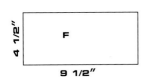

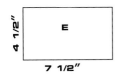

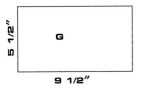

GREAT SHORTCUT BORDER TIP

Instead of cutting and piecing the four black border strips, cut one **20" × 24"** black block, then appliqué the completed quilt center to it.

PATCHES		
Fabric and Yardage	Number of Pieces	Shape
Assorted Tan Plaids and Stripes[1] ½ yd.	1	A
	2	B
	1	C
	1	D
	2	E
	1	F
	1	G

BORDER		
Fabric and Yardage	Number of Pieces	Size
Black Felt[2]	2	2¼″ × 20″
	2	2¼″ × 28″

[1] Reserve remainder of fabric for cutting border trim.
[2] Sizes include ¼″ seam allowance on edges that will be stitched and no seam allowance on remaining edges. Reserve remainder of felt for cutting appliqués.

APPLIQUÉS		
Fabric and Yardage	Number of Pieces	Size/Shape
Red Plaid[1] ½ yd.	2	Heart
Brown Plaid[2] ¼ yd.	1	Rectangle 4½″ × 6″
Black Felt[3]	1	Ark
	1	Tree
	1	Bird
	1	Animal #1
	1	Animal #2
	1	Animal #3
	1	Animal #4
	1	Animal #5
	1	Animal #6
	1	Animal #7

[1] Add ¼″ seam allowance.
[2] Do not use seam allowance.
[3] Use remainder of fabric from border. Do not add seam allowance.

Block

1. Sew patches together to make 4 units.

2. Arrange units as shown. Join units to make 2 rows. Join rows.

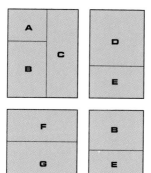

FINISHED BLOCK

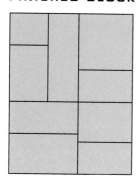

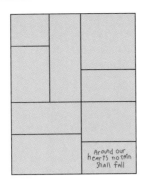

1. Transfer lettering pattern to lower right-hand corner patch (E), centered.
2. Use 2 strands black floss to backstitch lettering.

APPLIQUÉ

Note: See hand-appliqué stitches on page 77.

1. Prepare, arrange, and secure all appliqués on the block.

◆ *For heart:* Prepare fabric hearts for double appliqué; see below. Press.

2. Hand appliqué all shapes in place.

◆ *For ark:* Use 3 or more strands brown embroidery floss to stitch X's ¼" in from ark edges, all the way around.

◆ *For rectangle:* Do not turn edges under. Use 3 or more strands brown floss to stitch shape in place, making running stitch ¼" in from edges.

◆ *For heart:* Use 2 or 3 strands black floss to blanket-stitch heart in place.

◆ *For felt appliqués:* Use black thread to invisibly stitch shapes in place.

GREAT DOUBLE APPLIQUÉ TIP

1. Mark appliqué shape, including 1/4" seam allowance, on wrong side of fabric.
2. Place a piece of matching fabric behind marked piece, right sides together. Stitch on seam line all the way around. Do not leave an opening for turning.

3. Cut a small center slit in one layer of fabric (the one that will be the underside).
4. Cut out appliqué, adding 1/8" seam allowance to underside and 1/4" to top side.
5. Turn appliqué right side out through slit. Press.

6. Pin or glue center of appliqué to background fabric, both right side up.
7. Hand-sew the appliqué in place. (For added dimension, stuff appliqué through slit in underside before stitching in place.)

Border

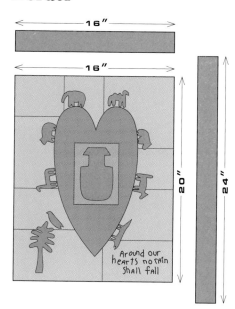

1. Join felt strips to quilt center, shorter pieces at top and bottom, then longer pieces at sides.

2. Cut six slits in each border side, perpendicular to border edges. Thread border trim through slits, one strip at a time, then knot ends on right side of quilt top to make one continuous strip all the way around quilt. Trim knot ends evenly or as desired.

Finishing

1. Cut batting 16″ × 20″. Cut brown felt 25″ × 29″ for backing.
2. Assemble quilt layers, centering batting and backing behind quilt top.
3. Use 2 or 3 strands black floss to blanket-stitch quilt layers together where block edges meet borders.
4. Trim backing to 1½″ beyond border. Cut right-triangle points to ½″ from border, making 9 points at top and bottom, 11 points at sides, and symmetrical corners.
5. Use black floss to stitch buttons on border between visible segments of tied strip, stitching through both quilt front and backing.
6. Use 2 or 3 strands black floss to stitch ½″-high X's randomly on quilt center. Do not stitch lettered patch.

Y ou may lose the primitive feeling of this design if you make it in primary or pastel colors, but you can certainly change the palette from warm to cool, or vary the placement or balance of light and dark tones. You might consider making the entire piece from solid colors—or even felt.

Around our hearts no rain shall fall

Photocopy this page, then create your own color scheme using colored pencils or markers. Refer to the examples shown, or design a unique color scheme to match your decor or please your fancy. Note how different palettes can make this design child-like or sophisticated.

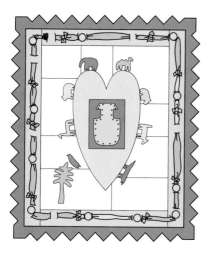

Flower and Bud Quilt

It is not likely that we will ever know the story behind this surprisingly sophisticated antique primitive with its oversized buds and the not-quite-symmetrical circle and star in the center that give it a slightly squashed look. It seems to have been cut freehand, paper-snowflake style. Is it a Whig Rose gone wild? A child's first attempt at appliqué? Was it meant to be the center of a full-size quilt? In any event, it is graphic, charming, and easy to re-create.

Note: All dimensions except for binding are finished size.

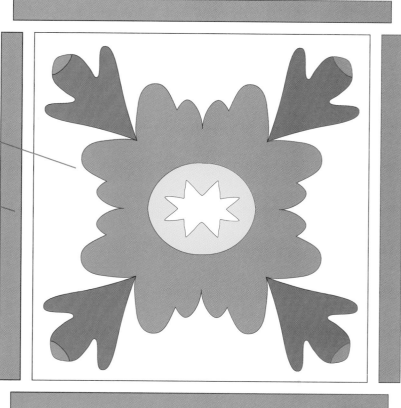

BLOCK

One block, 20″ square, with appliqués

BORDER

2 strips, 1¼″ x 20″, and 2 strips, 1¼″ × 22½″

BINDING

1¼″-wide strip, pieced as necessary and cut to size

*Note: All dimensions include ¼" seam allowance
unless otherwise stated.*

Yardages are based on 44" fabric. Enlarge and complete appliqué patterns on page 83, then prepare templates #1 through #5 for hand-appliqué; see also *Appliqué Tips*, page 76, and *Hand-Appliqué*, page 77. Cut block, strips, and appliqués following charts; see *Using the Cutting Charts*, pages 74 to 75. Cut binding as directed below. Strips include extra length unless otherwise stated.

DIMENSIONS

FINISHED BLOCK
20" square; about 28¾" diagonal

FINISHED QUILT
22½" square

MATERIALS

☐ **MUSLIN SOLID**
¾ yd.

☐ **YELLOW SOLID**
¼ yd.

▨ **RED SOLID**
1 yd.

▨ **BLUE SOLID**
¼ yd.

BINDING
Use ¼ yd. yellow solid to make a 1¼" × 110" strip. Reserve remainder of fabric for cutting appliqué #2.

BACKING *
1 yd.

BATTING *

THREAD

* Backing and batting should be cut and pieced as necessary so they are at least 4" larger on all sides than the quilt top, then trimmed to size after quilting.

Fabric and Yardage	Number of Pieces	Size/Shape
BLOCK		
Muslin Solid[1] ¾ yd.	1	23¼" square
BORDER		
Red Solid ¼ yd.	2	1¼" × 24"
	2	1¼" × 27"
APPLIQUÉS		
Muslin Solid[2]	1	#1
Yellow Solid[3]	1	#2
Red Solid ¾ yd.	1	#3
	4	#5
Blue Solid ¼ yd.	4	#4

[1] Use remainder of fabric for cutting appliqué #1.
[2] Use remainder of fabric from block.
[3] Use remainder of fabric from binding.

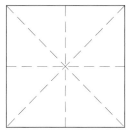

1. Mark guidelines for appliqué placement on quilt block.

◆ Mark horizontal and vertical center lines completely across block.

◆ Mark diagonal lines from corner to corner in both directions.

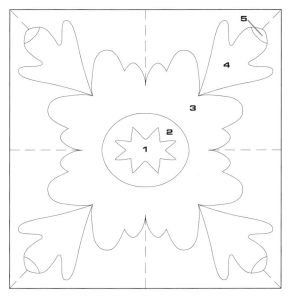

2. Prepare fabric shapes for hand-appliqué; see *Hand-Appliqué*, page 77.

◆ *For appliqués #2 and #3:* Do not turn inner edges under.

3. Arrange and secure all appliqués on block, starting in center with flower and working outward symmetrically, referring to marked guidelines.

◆ *For flower:* Assemble appliqués with #3 on the bottom and #1 on top, centering all pieces. Center assembled flower on block.

◆ *For leaf and bud:* Arrange bud (#5) either under or over leaf (#4).

4. Hand appliqué all shapes in place.

Border

Join border to quilt center, shorter strips at sides, then longer strips at top and bottom.

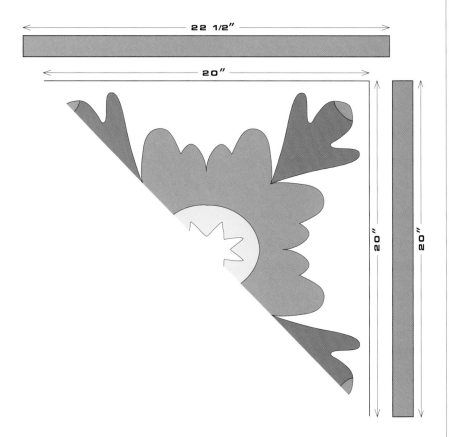

Finishing

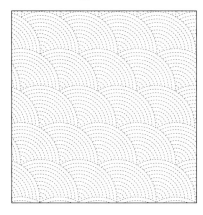

1. Mark allover quilting design on backing: Use a compass set for radius of 6¼″ to mark clam shell design on the diagonal. Mark additional curved lines ½″ apart for inward echo quilting.

2. Prepare batting and backing.

3. Assemble quilt layers.

4. Quilt on marked lines.

5. Trim batting and backing to ⅜″ beyond outermost seam line.

6. Bind quilt edges.

The Flower and Bud pattern has such graphic appeal, and is so easy to make, that you might consider using more or less of it to create a bigger or smaller quilt. All of the following dimensions indicate finished sizes.

1. Combine four blocks, converting the borders to sashing between them, to make a hanging 43 3/4" square.

2. Combine four blocks without sashing to make a 40" square. Place single buds within 5 3/4" squares, to make corner blocks. Join these to 40" × 5 3/4" borders embellished with additional buds. Join these to the four-block pieces to make a hanging 51 1/2" square.

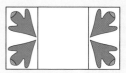

3. Place four buds on an 11 1/2" square to make a tilelike design. Join four of these to make a hanging 23" square —or make and arrange as many as you like to make a larger quilt. Consider what the effect would be if you made these blocks with alternating light and dark backgrounds.

4. Join two 5 3/4" borders to a panel of any length, and make a pillow, place mat, table runner or dresser scarf.

Achange of colors can give the Flower and Bud quilt a completely different feeling. You could use primary colors or make it in Christmas reds and greens. See what happens when you place light or bright colors on a dark background.

P hotocopy this page, then create your own color scheme using colored pencils or markers. Refer to the examples shown, or design a unique color scheme to match your decor or please your fancy.

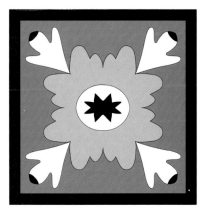

Rose and Grapes Quilt

BY EDITH OLBRICH
HAND-QUILTED BY LILLIAN OLSEN

Beginners, take heart. This exquisite quilt was Edith Olbrich's first appliqué piece, and she and her aunt, who quilted it, are justifiably proud of the ten years they invested in it. The rose-and-grape-cluster design is a reproduction of an antique and requires more time than expertise. If the quilt is too large for your wall or too ambitious for your schedule, make just one block and finish it with the border.

Note: All dimensions except for binding are finished size.
Amounts for pillow/small wallhanging are given in parentheses.

BINDING
1½″-wide strip, pieced as necessary and cut to size

BLOCK
4 (1) blocks, 23″ square, with appliqués

BORDER
4 strips, 3½″ × 46″ (3½″ × 23″)

CORNER SQUARE
Four 3½″ corner square

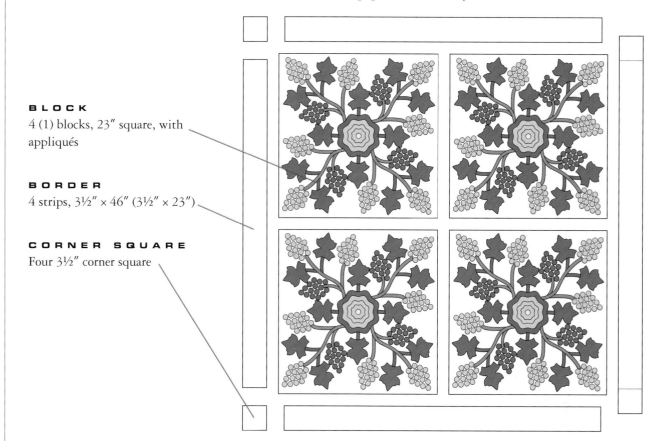

GREAT EDGE-TURNING TIP

Use the following technique to make smoothly turned edges on round or nearly round appliqués.

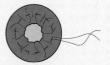

1. From thin cardboard, cut out a template the size of the finished appliqué.
2. Cut out the appliqué from fabric, including 1/4″ seam allowance.
3. Baste a line of small even running stitches around the edge of the appliqué, leaving long thread ends; do not secure thread.

4. Center the template on the wrong side of the appliqué, and pull thread ends to gather fabric tautly over cardboard.
5. Press appliqué to crease fold at edge.
6. Remove template and basting. Flatten appliqué.

*Note: All dimensions include ¼" seam allowance
unless otherwise stated.*

Yardages are based on 44" fabric. Sizes and amounts for pillow/small wallhanging are given in parentheses. Complete partial patterns on page 85, then prepare templates #1 through #7 for hand-appliqué; see also *Appliqué Tips*, page 76, and *Hand-Appliqué*, page 77. Cut block, strips, and appliqués following charts; see *Using the Cutting Charts*, pages 74 to 75. Cut binding and stems as directed below. Strips include extra length, unless otherwise stated.

DIMENSIONS

FINISHED BLOCK
23" square; about 32½" diagonal

FINISHED QUILT
53" (30") square

MATERIALS

☐ **MUSLIN SOLID**
5 (2) yds.

☐ **PALE YELLOW SOLID**
¼ yd.

☐ **PALE PEACH SOLID**
¼ yd.

☐ **PINK PRINT**
¾ (¼) yd.

☐ **DK. GREEN SOLID**
1 (¼) yd.

☐ **DK. BROWN SOLID**
¼ yd.

BINDING
Use ½ yd. muslin solid to make a 1½" × 220" (1½" × 100") strip.

LEAF STEMS
Use ¼ yd. dark green solid to cut a ¾" × 200" (¾" × 50") bias strip.

GRAPE STEMS
Use ¼ yd. dark brown solid to cut a ¾" × 300" (¾" × 80") bias strip.

BACKING*
3½ (1¼) yds.

BATTING*

THREAD

EMBROIDERY FLOSS
One skein dark green

*Backing and batting should be cut and pieced as necessary so they are at least 4" larger on all sides than the quilt top, then trimmed to size after quilting.

BLOCKS			
Fabric and Yardage	Number of Pieces		Size
	For 4 (1) Blocks	For 4 Corner Squares	
Muslin Solid 2¾ (¾) yds.	4 (1)	–	23½" square
	–	4	4" square

APPLIQUÉS		
Fabric and Yardage	Number of Pieces	Shape
Dk. Green Solid 1 (¼) yds.	4 (1)	#1
	48 (12)	#6
	240 (60)	#7
Pink Print ¾ (¼) yd.	4 (1)	#2
	4 (1)	#4
	480 (120)	#7
Pale Peach Solid ¼ yd.	4 (1)	#3
Pale Yellow Solid ¼ yd.	4 (1)	#5

BORDER		
Fabric and Yardage	Number of Pieces	Size¹
Muslin Solid 1½ (½) yds.	4	4" × 46½" (4" × 23½")
¹ Exact length		

ADJUSTING THE SIZE

The size of this quilt can be adjusted easily for a pillow/small wallhanging by joining the border to a single block. Refer to the cutting charts, above, for the number and sizes of pieces to cut for the different sizes.

QUILT
4 blocks in a 2 × 2 layout

PILLOW/SMALL WALLHANGING
1 block

1. Mark guidelines for appliqué placement on each quilt block.

♦ Mark horizontal and vertical center lines completely across block.

♦ Mark diagonal lines from corner to corner in both directions.

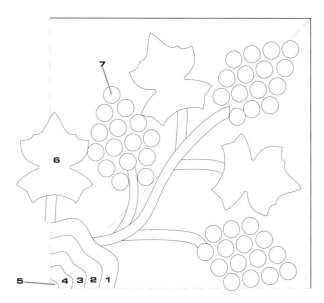

2. Prepare fabric shapes for hand-appliqué; see *Hand-Appliqué*, page 77.

♦ *For appliqués #1 through #4:* Do not turn inner edges under .

♦ *For stems:* Prepare bias strips/tubes ¼″ wide (finished width), referring to *Stems/Vines*, page 76.

3. Arrange and secure all appliqués on each block, starting in center with flower and working outward symmetrically, referring to marked guidelines.

♦ *For flower:* Assemble appliqués, with #1 on bottom and #5 on top, centering all pieces. Center assembled flower on block.

♦ *For grapes:* Arrange bunches of 15 grapes each.

♦ *For stems:* Use bias strips/tubes to make 48 (12) green leaf stems and 48 (12) brown grape stems.

4. Hand appliqué all shapes in place.

♦ *For appliqué #7 (grapes):* Use needleturned-edge method of appliqué (page 77) and insert a tiny amount of fiberfill under each grape before completing stitching.

Quilt Center

Arrange blocks for 4-block quilt as shown. Join blocks to form 2 rows. Join rows.

Border

Join two corner squares to two side strips. Join strips to quilt center, plain strips at top and bottom, then pieced strips at sides.

QUILT

PILLOW/SMALL WALLHANGING

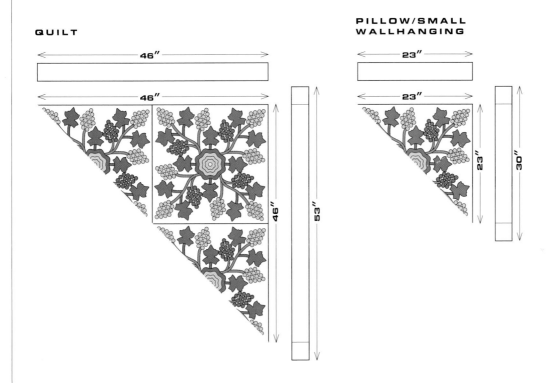

Finishing

Varying amounts and directions for pillow/small wall-hanging are given in parentheses.

EACH QUILT BLOCK

1. Mark quilting designs on quilt top.
- *For appliqués:* Mark veins on leaves (#6).

♦ *For quilt center background:* Mark 45° diagonal lines across quilt in one direction, ⅝″ apart; do not mark lines on appliqués.

QUILT BORDER

PILLOW/SMALL WALLHANGING BORDER

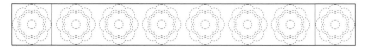

♦ *For border:* Use actual-size pattern on page 85 to mark 13 (7) border flowers on each border strip, beginning at center of each strip and working outward to ends. Mark one flower on each corner square.

2. Prepare batting and backing.

3. Assemble layers for quilting.

4. Quilt in-the-ditch around all appliqués. Quilt on all marked lines.

5. Mark guidelines for grape tendrils on quilt center, then embroider: Use 2 strands dark green floss to work tendrils with tiny outline stitches (see embroidery stitch details on page 77), making sure stitches do not show through on quilt back.

6. Trim batting and backing to ½″ beyond outermost seam line.

7. Bind quilt edges. (Add back for pillow, then stuff with fiberfill.)

Y ou can choose any palette you like for a traditional appliqué pattern such as this one. For a painted effect use several related hues in each bunch of grapes, or use prints as Polly Whitehorn did for her Theorem Fruit Bowl on page 48.

Photocopy this page, then create your own color scheme using colored pencils or markers. Refer to the examples shown, or design a unique color scheme to match your decor or please your fancy.

Theorem Fruit Bowl Quilt

BY POLLY WHITEHORN

The design for this charming quilt is based on traditional theorem paintings of the late eighteenth and early nineteenth centuries, popular with well-bred ladies of the times. Polly Whitehorn's clever use of print fabrics captures the subtle effect of the stenciling technique used on them. This small quilt with its picture-frame border won first place in the wallhanging category at the Eastern Long Island Quilter's Society show in 1992.

Note: All dimensions except for binding are finished size.

BLOCK
One block, 19″ × 14″,
with appliqués

BORDER
2 strips, 2″ × 14″,
and 2 strips, 2″ × 19″

CORNER SQUARE
Four 2″ corner squares

BINDING
1¼″-wide strip, pieced
as necessary and cut to size

Note: All dimensions include ¼" seam allowance
unless otherwise stated.

Yardages are based on 44" fabric. Complete bowl half-pattern on page 85, then use it and actual-size patterns on pages 86 and 87 to prepare templates #1 through #31 for hand-appliqué; see also *Appliqué Tips*, page 76, and *Hand-Appliqué*, page 77. Cut block, strips, and appliqués following charts; see *Using the Cutting Charts*, page 74. Cut binding and stems as directed below. Strips include extra length, unless otherwise stated.

DIMENSIONS

FINISHED BLOCK
19" × 14"

FINISHED QUILT
23" × 18"

MATERIALS

MUSLIN SOLID
½ yd.

ASSORTED YELLOW ❖
¼ yd.

TAN PRINT
¼ yd.

ASSORTED ORANGE ❖
¼ yd.

ASSORTED PINK ❖
¼ yd.

ASSORTED RED ❖
¼ yd.

DK. RED PRINT
½ yd.

ASSORTED GREEN ❖
¼ yd.

ASSORTED OLIVE ❖
¼ yd.

ASSORTED PURPLE ❖
¼ yd.

NAVY PRINT
½ yd.

BLACK SOLID
¼ yd.

BINDING
¼ yd. navy print is cut and pieced to make a 1¼" × 100" strip. Reserve remainder of fabric for cutting appliqué #27.

STEMS
Use ¼ yd. green solid to cut a ⅜" × 30" bias strip (includes ⅛" seam allowance).

BACKING *
¾ yd.

BATTING *

THREAD

EMBROIDERY FLOSS
One skein each green and black

❖ Use an assortment of solids, prints, and florals, ¼ yd. total for each color.

* Backing and batting should be cut and pieced as necessary so they are at least 4" larger on all sides than the quilt top, then trimmed to size after quilting.

APPLIQUÉS		
Fabric and Yardage	Number of Pieces	Shape
Yellow ¼ yd.	1	#10
	1	#21
	1	#22
	1	#24
	10	#28
	1	#29
	1	#31
Tan Print ¼ yd.	1	#9
Orange[1] ¼ yd.	1	#12
	1	#30
Pink ¼ yd.	1	#2
	1	#13
	1	#14
Red ¼ yd.	3	#6
	3	#8
	1	#11
	1	#18
Dk. Red Print[2]	1	#17
Green ¼ yd.	1	#1
	1	#3
	4	#4
	1	#5
	1	#5$_R$
	1	#16
	1	#19
	4	#20[3]
Olive ¼ yd.	3	#7
	4	#4
	1	#23
	1	#25
	1	#26

APPLIQUÉS		
Fabric and Yardage	Number of Pieces	Shape
Purple ¼ yd.	21	#6[4]
Navy Print[5]	1	#27
Black Solid ¼ yd.	6	#15

[1] Reserve remainder of fabric for cutting corner squares.
[2] Use remainder of fabric from border.
[3] Cut 1 from first fabric, 2 from second fabric.
[4] Cut 3 from first fabric, 8 from second fabric, 10 from third fabric.
[5] Use remainder of fabric from binding.
Note: Subscript $_R$ denotes reversed shape.

BLOCKS			
	Number of Pieces		
Fabric and Yardage	For 1 Block	For 4 Corner Squares	Size
Muslin ½ yd.	1	—	19½″ × 14½″
Orange*	—	4	2½″ square

*Use remainder of one fabric from appliqués #12 and #13.

BORDER		
Fabric and Yardage	Number of Pieces	Size (exact length)
Dk. Red ½ yd.	2	2½″ × 14½″
	2	2½″ × 19½″

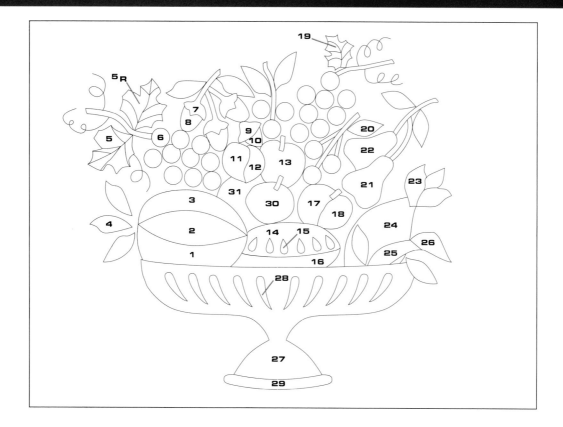

1. Mark guidelines for appliqué placement on quilt block.
- Center appliqué pattern #27/#28/#29 (bowl) widthwise on block, ⅝″ up from bottom 19″ edge, and transfer outlines.
- Use fruit pattern to mark remaining outlines.

2. Prepare fabric shapes for hand appliqué; see *Hand-Appliqué*, page 77.
- *For bowl:* Prepare 10 individual #28 appliqués for layering on top of #27; or see the *Great Appliqué Tip*, page 53.
- *For stems:* Prepare green bias strip/tube ⅜″ wide (finished width), referring to *Stems/Vines*, page 76.

3. Arrange and secure all fabric shapes on block, aligning outlines of fabric shapes and guidelines.
- *For stems:* Use bias strip/tube to make stems, following actual-size pattern for lengths.

4. Hand appliqué all shapes in place.

Border

Join corner squares to side border strips. Join border to quilt center, plain strips at top and bottom, then pieced strips at sides.

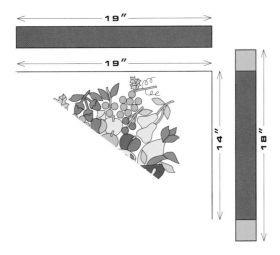

Finishing

1. Mark quilting designs on quilt front.

◆ *For appliqués:* Mark veins on #s 5, 19 and 23 (leaves).

◆ *For background:* Mark 45° diagonal lines across quilt center in one direction, alternately spacing pairs of lines ¼″ and ½″ apart; do not mark lines on appliqués.

2. Prepare batting and backing.

3. Assemble layers for quilting.

4. Quilt in-the-ditch around all appliqués. Quilt on all marked lines.

5. Mark guidelines for tendrils on quilt center, then embroider: Use 2 strands black floss to work tendrils with tiny outline stitches (see stitch detail, page 77), making sure stitches do not show through on quilt back.

6. Trim batting and backing to ⅜″ beyond outermost seam line.

7. Bind quilt edges.

GREAT APPLIQUÉ TIP

Cut out the accent shapes (#28) from the bowl appliqué (#27) to make 10 openings. For reverse appliqué, turn under the edges of the openings, baste a solid piece of accent fabric behind the bowl, then slipstitch around the openings. Arrange and appliqué the assembled bowl/accents in place on the quilt block.

Y ou can make the Theorem Fruit Bowl as bright or as subdued as you wish, or choose your colors to reflect a holiday or season. Traditional theorem painting is often done on dark-colored velvet so, if you are sure of your appliqué skills, you might consider using velveteen for the base fabric.

Photocopy this page, then create your own color scheme using colored pencils or markers. Refer to the examples shown, or design a unique color scheme to match your decor or please your fancy. If you use solid rather than print fabrics, your quilt will have a more graphic effect.

Whig Rose Quilt

Perhaps this lively antique rendition of the Whig Rose once graced
a nineteenth-century crib. Notice that the square design was very
effectively lengthened with pieced Flying Geese borders at the top and bottom.
A close look reveals that the appliquéd block is quilted with rose, heart, diamond,
and even embroidery scissors motifs, which add a depth of texture to this charming
traditional pattern.

Note: All dimensions except for binding are finished size.

BINDING
1″-wide strip, pieced as necessary and cut to size

BLOCK
One block, 26″ square, with appliqués

FIRST BORDER
4 strips, 1½″ wide, cut to size

SECOND BORDER
4 strips, 3″ wide, cut to size

THIRD BORDER
4 strips, 1½″ wide, cut to size

FOURTH BORDER
2 pieced strips, 4″ × 38″

FIFTH BORDER
2 strips, 2″ wide, cut to size

Note: All dimensions include ¼″ seam allowance
unless otherwise stated.

Yardages are based on 44″ fabric. Complete partial patterns on page 88, then prepare templates #1 through #8 for hand-appliqué; see also *Appliqué Tips*, page 76, and *Hand-Appliqué*, page 77. Cut blocks, strips, and appliqués following charts; see *Using the Cutting Charts*, page 74 to 75. Cut binding and stems as directed below. Strips include extra length unless otherwise stated. (NOTE: Angles on all patches are either 45° or 90°.)

DIMENSIONS

FINISHED BLOCK
26″ square; about 36¾″ diagonal

FINISHED QUILT
38″ × 50″

MATERIALS

☐ **MUSLIN SOLID**
1½ yds.

☐ **YELLOW SOLID**
¼ yd.

☐ **PINK SOLID**
¼ yd.

■ **RED SOLID**
1¼ yds.

■ **GREEN SOLID**
2¼ yds.

BINDING
Use ¼ yd. red solid to cut and piece a 1″ × 200″ strip.

STEMS
Use ¼ yd. green solid to cut and piece a ¾″ × 100″ bias strip.

BACKING *
2¾ yds.

BATTING *

THREAD

* Backing and batting should be cut and pieced as necessary so they are at least 4″ larger on all sides than the quilt top, then trimmed to size after quilting.

CUTTING SCHEMATICS
(Seam allowance included)

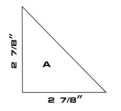

2 7/8″ · 2 7/8″ · A

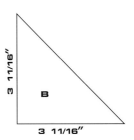

3 11/16″ · 3 11/16″ · B

| FIRST CUT | | | SECOND CUT | | |
| | | | Number of Pieces | | |
Fabric and Yardage	Number of Pieces	Size	For Block	For Fourth Border	Size/Shape
BLOCK AND PATCHES					
Muslin 1 yd.	1	$26\frac{1}{2}" \times 40"$	1	–	$26\frac{1}{2}"$ square
	3	$2\frac{7}{8}" \times 40"$	–	76	A
Red ¼ yd.	1	$3^{11}/_{16}" \times 40"$	–	18	B
Green ¼ yd.	3	$3^{11}/_{16}" \times 40"$	–	20	B

Fabric and Yardage	Number of Pieces	Size
Red[1] ½ yd.	**FIRST BORDER**	
	4	$2" \times 33"$
Muslin ½ yd.	**SECOND BORDER**	
	4	$3\frac{1}{2}" \times 39"$
Green[1] 1½ yd.	**THIRD BORDER**	
	4	$2" \times 42"$
	FIFTH BORDER	
	2	$2\frac{1}{2}" \times 42"$

[1] Reserve remainder of fabric for cutting appliqués.

Fabric and Yardage	Number of Pieces	Shape
APPLIQUÉS		
Yellow ¼ yd.	1	#1
	8	#6
Pink ¼ yd.	12	#3
Red[2] ¼ yd.	1	#2
	12	#4
	8	#7
Green[2] ¼ yd.	4	#5
	16	#8

[2] Use remainder of fabric from borders.

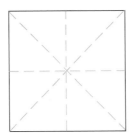

1. Mark guidelines for appliqué placement on quilt block. Mark horizontal and vertical center lines completely across block. Mark diagonal lines from corner to corner in both directions.

2. Prepare fabric shapes for hand-appliqué; see *Hand-Appliqué*, page 77.

- *For appliqués #1 and #6, and for bottom edges of #5:* Do not turn edges under.
- *For appliqués #2 and #7:* Cut away center.
- *For appliqués #3 and #4:* Prepare all petals individually, or see the *Great Appliqué Tip* below. Do not turn bottom edges under.
- *For stems:* Prepare green bias strip/tube ¼" wide (finished width), referring to *Stems/Vines*, page 76.

GREAT APPLIQUÉ TIP

Use the completed pattern for the large flower to cut a solid ring of red petals (#4) instead of 12 individual petals. Prepare the ring for appliqué and secure it on the block over the green petals (#5) before adding individual pink petals (#3) and the flower center (#1/#2).

3. Arrange and secure all appliqués on block, starting with center flower and working outward symmetrically, referring to marked guidelines. Cut out centers of #s 2 and 7; turn center edges under.

- ◆ *For large flower:* Arrange #5's on background. Arrange #4's on top, then #3's. Baste #1 behind #2, centered. Baste #1/#2 in place, centered.
- ◆ *For stems:* Use bias strip/tube to make 4 short stems and 4 long stems.
- ◆ *For small flowers:* Baste #6's behind #7's, centered. Arrange assembled flowers on background.

4. Hand appliqué all shapes in place.

Borders

1. Join first, second, and third borders to all four quilt sides, mitering corners.

2. For fourth border, sew 2 A's to each B. Join units, alternating colors of B's, to make two 19-unit strips. Join strips to quilt top and bottom.

3. Join fifth border to quilt top and bottom.

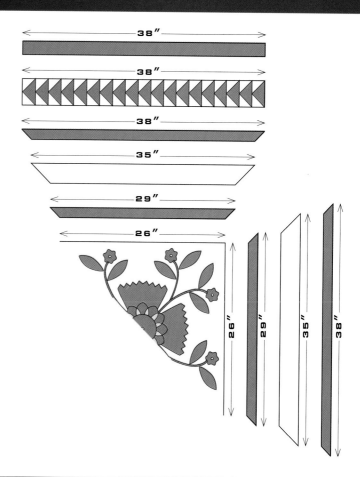

Finishing

1. Complete actual-size quilting motifs on page 88 and use to prepare templates (or use cookie cutter shapes; see the *Great Template Tip*, page 63).

2. Mark quilting designs on quilt top.
- *For **quilt center:*** Mark scissors, flowers, hearts, and diamonds (or other simple shapes) on background, arranging them between appliqués. Mark shapes for either single- or double-outline quilting.

- *For **first, second, and third borders:*** Mark allover grid, making lines parallel to and perpendicular to mitered corner seams, 1″ apart.
- *For **fifth border:*** Center and mark 1″-wide diamonds on each strip.

3. Prepare batting and backing.

4. Assemble quilt layers.

5. Quilt on marked lines. Quilt ¼″ inside edges of appliqués #2 through #8. Quilt additional straight lines on appliqués #2 and #5.

6. Trim batting and backing to ¼″ beyond outermost seam line.

7. Bind quilt edges.

Note: All dimensions are finished size.

You can make a Whig Rose pillow or small wallhanging by reducing the number and/or size of the components. If you reduce the appliqués 50%, stitch them on a 13" background, and add a single 1 1/2"-wide border on all four sides, you will have a 16" square, just the right size for a pillow front. Assemble the layers, quilt them, add a pillow back, then quick stuff with a 16"-square knife-edge pillow form.

For a half-size (19" × 25") wallhanging, reduce the size of all quilt pieces 50% and assemble them in the same manner as for the full-size wallhanging, or omit the binding and display the wallhanging in a frame.

PILLOW

SMALL
WALLHANGING

Try using cookie cutters as templates for simple appliqué shapes or quilting motifs. They come in all sizes and shapes, and are sturdy enough to last for years.

If the shapes are to be used for appliqué, add seam allowance as needed around the edges when cutting them out. If they are to be used for quilting, you can mark additional outlines 1/8" to 1/4" apart on the fabric for double-outline or echo quilting.

The antique Whig Rose quilt owes much of its impact to its limited palette—there are really only two colors on the muslin background. Experiment to see how the effect is softened if you add more colors, or a try a background with less contrast.

Photocopy this page, then create your own color scheme using colored pencils or markers. Refer to the examples shown, or design a unique color scheme to match your decor or please your fancy.

Bears, Bears Everywhere

BY SONYA LEE BARRINGTON

This quilt was inspired by a book the designer read to her children when they were small. She divided the design space diagonally in both directions to make four triangular areas, then created a different teddy bear scene in each, working the appliqués with pearl cotton and perfect running stitches. We've given this piece the Expert's rank not because it requires great experience but because the four scenes have so many pieces to cut, arrange, and embellish.

Note: All dimensions except binding are finished size.

BLOCK

One block, 41″ × 56″, with appliqués

BINDING

1½″-wide strip, pieced as necessary and cut to size

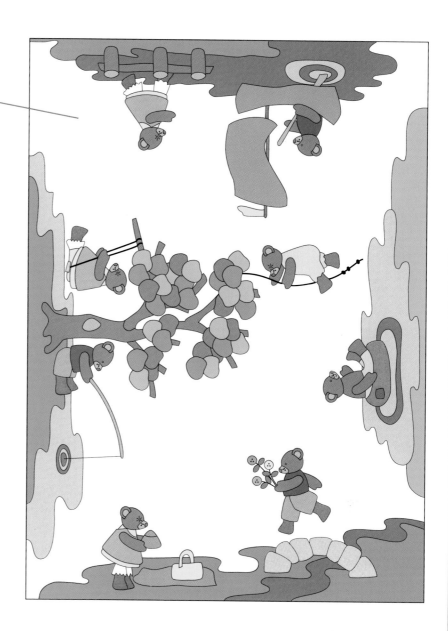

*Note: All dimensions include ¼" seam allowance
unless otherwise stated.*

Yardages are based on 44" fabric. Enlarge patterns on page 96, then prepare templates #1 through #64 for hand-appliqué using actual-size patterns on pages 89 to 95; see also *Appliqué Tips*, page 76, and *Hand-Appliqué*, page 77. Cut block and appliqués following chart; see *Using the Cutting Charts*, pages 74 to 75. Cut binding as directed below.

DIMENSIONS

FINISHED BLOCK
41" × 56"

FINISHED QUILT
41" × 56"

MATERIALS

MUSLIN SOLID
1¾ yds.

YELLOW SOLID
¼ yd.

YELLOW FLORAL
¼ yd.

TAN SOLID
¼ yd.

RED-BROWN SOLID
¼ yd.

RED-BROWN FLORAL
¼ yd.

BROWN SOLID
¼ yd.

LT. BLUE SOLID
¼ yd.

ROYAL BLUE SOLID
¼ yd.

LT. GREEN SOLID
¼ yd.

LT. GREEN FLORAL
¼ yd.

DK. GREEN SOLID
¼ yd.

DK. GREEN FLORAL
¾ yd.

MED. PURPLE SOLID
¼ yd.

MED. PURPLE FLORAL
¼ yd.

DK. PURPLE FLORAL
¼ yd.

BLACK SOLID
¼ yd.

GRAY SOLID
¼ yd.

BINDING
Use ¼ yd. dk. green floral to cut and piece a 1½" × 210" bias strip.

BACKING *
1¾ yds.

BATTING *

THREAD

PEARL COTTON
One ball #8 to match each fabric

EYELET TRIM
¼ yd. pre-gathered off-white eyelet trim, 1" wide

GREAT PLAN-AHEAD TIP

This quilt will look best if the background is cut in one piece. Your fabric must be at least 41 1/2" wide after preshrinking. If you have any doubts about the fabric you plan to use, buy a small piece and test it. Fabrics generally shrink more on the lengthwise grain than the crosswise, so most that come in 44" widths should be adequate; muslin and sheeting are often available in wider widths.

*Backing and batting should be cut and pieced as necessary so they are at least 4" larger on all sides than the quilt top, then trimmed to size after quilting.

Fabric and Yardage	Number of Pieces	Size/Shape
BLOCK		
Muslin Solid 1¾ yds.	1	41½″ × 56½″
APPLIQUÉS		
Yellow Solid ¼ yd.	1	#21
	1	#22
	1	#49
	1	#59
Yellow Floral ¼ yd.	1	#14
	2	#14$_R$
	1	#26
Tan Solid ¼ yd.	4	#11
	4	#11$_R$
	4	#13
	4	#13$_R$
	3	#42
	1	#47
	1	#54
	1	#61
Red Brown Solid ¼ yd.	1	#17
	1	#18
	1	#33
	1	#46
Red Brown Floral ¼ yd.	1	#20
	1	#26
	1	#50
Brown Solid ¼ yd.	4	#10
	4	#10$_R$
	7	#16
	7	#16$_R$
	4	#12
	4	#12$_R$
	2	#19
	2	#19$_R$
	1	#23
	1	#40
	3	#41
	1	#53
	1	#55
	1	#56
	1	#57
Lt. Blue Solid ¼ yd.	1	#29
	1	#31
	1	#43
	1	#45
	1	#51
	1	#63

Fabric and Yardage	Number of Pieces	Size/Shape
APPLIQUÉS		
Royal Blue Solid ¼ yd.	1	#2
	1	#30
	1	#39
	1	#44
	1	#62
	1	#64
Lt. Green Solid ¼ yd.	12	#58
Lt. Green Floral ¼ yd.	1	#34
	1	#35
	1	#36
	1	#37
Dk. Green Solid ¼ yd.	6	#27
	12	#58
Dk. Green Floral ¼ yd.	1	#1
	1	#28
	1	#38
	1	#52
	12	#58
Med. Purple Solid ¼ yd.	1	#24
	1	#24$_R$
	1	#25
Med. Purple Floral ¼ yd.	1	#15
	2	#15$_R$
	1	#26
Dk. Purple Floral ¼ yd.	1	#23
	1	#23$_R$
Gray Solid ¼ yd.	1	#3
	1	#4
	1	#5
	1	#6
	1	#7
	1	#8
	1	#9
	1	#60
Black Solid ¼ yd.	4	#19
	5	#19$_R$
	1	#32
	1	#48

Note: Subscript $_R$ indicates reversed shape.

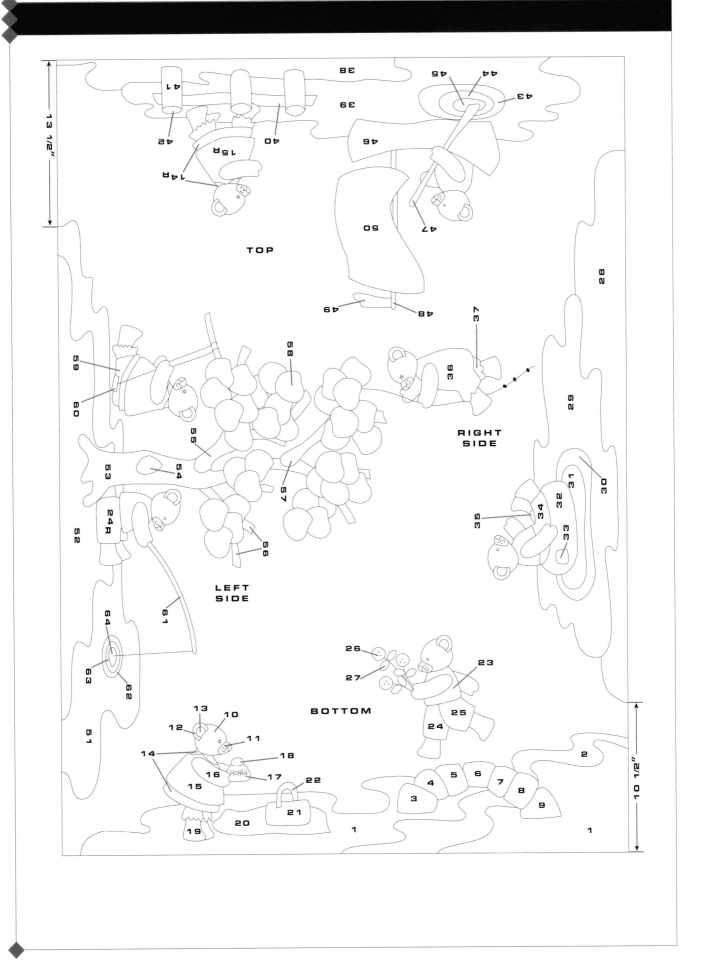

1. Prepare fabric shapes for hand-appliqué; see *Hand-Appliqué*, page 77.

2. Arrange and secure all appliqués on block, starting with background pieces and proceeding toward foreground.

- Secure grass (#1, #28, #38, #52) on each block side first, aligning straight edges of appliqués and block, and measuring in from corners for placement.

- Arrange water, bridge, and pier, then add blanket, basket, and tree with leaves, referring to drawing and photograph for placement.

- Arrange bears, clothing, and remaining motifs.

- *For pantaloons:* For each pantaloon leg, cut a 2″ length of eyelet trim and press under ⅛″ at ends. Secure on block with upper edge lapped by girl bear's dress bottom.

3. Hand appliqué all shapes in place.

- Use one strand matching pearl cotton to work tiny running stitches as close to appliqué edges as possible. Or use sewing thread and tiny invisible appliqué stitches, if you prefer.

GREAT APPLIQUÉ TIP

Use the actual-size patterns to cut each shape as indicated on the chart, adding seam allowance as desired. If, as you overlap and arrange the pieces, the layers seem bulky, cut away any parts that do not show. You can do this as you work, trimming the excess as you pin or stitch. Or, you can wait until your appliqué is complete, and remove the excess from the wrong side.

ACTUAL-SIZE PATTERNS

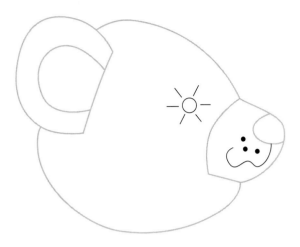

1. Mark lines for embroidery details on block and appliqués either freehand or by transferring actual-size patterns.

- Mark ropes for swinging and climbing bears.
- Mark fishing line and flower stems.
- Mark three dots for flower centers on each flower.
- Mark lettering on honey pot.
- Mark facial features on bears, adding eyelashes for girl bears only.

2. Use one strand pearl cotton to work all embroidery; see stitch details, below.

- Use tan to work ropes and fishing rod in backstitch; work knots on climbing rope in satin stitch.
- Use dark green to work outline stitch flower stems.
- Use yellow to work satin stitch eyes and French knot flower centers.
- Use black to work honey pot lettering and bears' smile in outline stitch, nose in satin stitch, freckles in seed stitch, and girl bears' eyelashes in straight stitch.

EMBROIDERY STITCHES

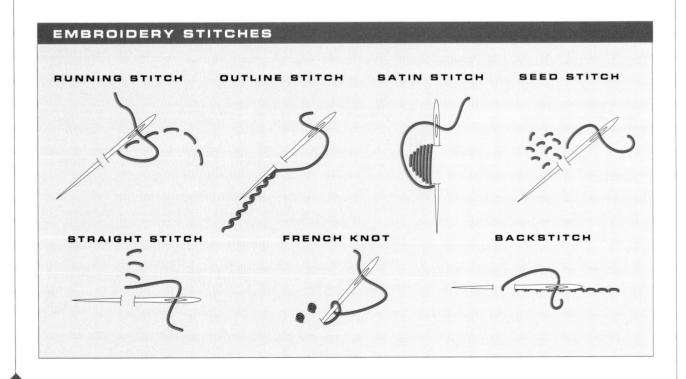

RUNNING STITCH OUTLINE STITCH SATIN STITCH SEED STITCH

STRAIGHT STITCH FRENCH KNOT BACKSTITCH

Finishing

1. Mark quilting lines on quilt top: Mark a grid of 4″ squares all over background, making lines parallel to quilt edges. Do not mark lines on appliqués.

2. Prepare batting and backing.

3. Assemble layers for quilting.

4. Use one strand off-white pearl cotton to quilt background on all marked lines and in-the-ditch around main appliqué outlines.

5. Mark rounded seam lines at corners of quilt top.

6. Trim batting and backing to ¾″ beyond quilt top seam line.

7. Bind quilt edges.

CHANGING COLORS

Photocopy this page, then create your own color scheme using colored pencils or markers.

Appendix

The sample cutting charts and schematics below demonstrate how these elements work together to provide the information needed to cut most of the pieces for any quilt project in the Better Homes and Gardens® Creative Quilting Collection volumes. Any additional cuts, such as for binding, can be found in the Fabric and Cutting List for each project.

DRAFTING SCHEMATIC

Drafting schematics, which do not include seam allowance, are provided for your convenience as an aid in preparing templates.

DRAFTING SCHEMATIC

(No seam allowance added)

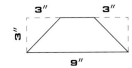

CUTTING SCHEMATIC

Cutting schematics, which do include seam allowance, can be used for preparing templates (with seam allowance included) but are given primarily as an aid for speed-cutting shapes using a rotary cutter and special rulers with angles marked on them.

CUTTING SCHEMATICS

(Seam allowance included)

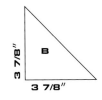

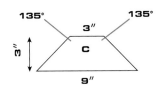

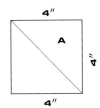

FABRIC AND YARDAGE

This column gives the color and amount of fabric needed to cut groups of shapes, rounded up to the next ¼ yard. To change the color scheme of a project, refer to the dimensions given for individual groups of shapes and use (combine them as needed) to calculate the new yardage.

FIRST CUT

Cut the number of pieces in the sizes indicated on either the lengthwise or crosswise grain unless otherwise stated, using templates or rotary cutting rulers. For 40″-long strips, cutting completely across the width of the fabric usually provides the most economical cuts.

SECOND CUT

Cut the number of pieces in the sizes and/or shapes indicated, referring to the cutting schematics for angles and cut sizes. Reversed pieces are designated by a subscript $_R$ (e.g., the reverse of a B patch is designated B_R) and can frequently be obtained from the same strips as their mirror images by cutting the two shapes alternately.

BORDER

From ½ yd. blue check cut two 2½″ × 29″ and two 2½″ × 32″ border strips.

FOOTNOTE

Use the cited instructions for Speedy Triangle Squares and mark the grids in the layout indicated.

APPLIQUÉS

From ¼ yd. red floral cut 16 flowers and 8 buds. From ¼ yd. blue floral cut 56 leaves. Reversed pieces are designated by a subscript $_R$ and these patterns should be turned over before marking onto fabric.

8 RED SOLID A'S

From ¼ yd. red solid, cut one 3⅞″ × 20″ strip. From strip cut four 3⅞″ squares. Cut squares in half to make 8 right-triangle A's.

6 WHITE SOLID C'S

From ¼ yd. white solid cut one 3½″ × 40″ strip. From strip cut six trapezoids.

FOOTNOTE REFERENCE

See the footnote underneath the chart for additional information about cutting this group of shapes.

	FIRST CUT		SECOND CUT	
Fabric and Yardage	Number of Pieces	Size	Number of Pieces	Shape
PLAIN PATCHES				
Red Solid ¼ yd.	1	3⅞″ × 20″	8	A
	1	3½″ × 40″	8	B
White Solid ¼ yd.	1	3⅞″ × 20″	8	A
	1	3½″ × 40″	6	C
SPEEDY TRIANGLE SQUARES				
Red Solid and White Solid ½ yd. each	2	16½″ × 20⅝″	72	B/B[1]
BORDER				
Blue Check ½ yd.	2	2½″ × 29″		
	2	2½″ × 32″		

[1] See Speedy Triangle Squares (page 93). Mark 4 × 5 grids with 3⅞″ squares.

APPLIQUÉS		
Fabric and Yardage	Number of Pieces	Shape
Red Floral ¼ yd.	16	Flower
	8	Bud
Blue Floral ¼ yd.	56	Leaf

Refer as well to Great Quiltmaking: All the Basics, *the detailed companion to the volumes in the Better Homes and Gardens® Creative Quilting Collection.*

Patterns and Templates

Whether you use solid or window templates, be sure always to mark the seam line of the appliqué. The cutting line can be omitted, if you prefer, and the shape cut out with the width of the seam allowance judged by eye.

It isn't always necessary to mark placement lines on the background piece, but when it is, mark them on the right side of the fabric; do not add seam allowance.

Seam Allowance

The appliqué patterns in this book do not include seam allowance. The width of the seam allowance on your appliqués is a matter of personal choice and practicality. Some people use ⅛" seam allowance on all of their appliqué shapes, while others prefer the same ¼" width they use for patchwork. Some add ⅛" seam allowance on small shapes or complex edges and allow ¼" for larger pieces with straight or gently curved edges. Still others tailor the width of their seam allowance to the needs of the particular appliqué methods they use.

Stems/Vines

Most appliquéd stems and vines are curved, so cut strips for them on the bias (adding seam allowance on long edges) to provide the flexibility they need. The seam allowance of the long edges of a strip can be pressed under or stitched together, right side out, to form a tube. Press the tube flat with the seam allowance pressed open on the back (or press it to one side if you want your stem/vine to have more dimension). Trim the seam allowance as needed so it doesn't show on the front.

Cut strips or tubes into the desired lengths before appliqué or cut them to size as they are sewn in place. Pin or baste carefully to assure that curves are smooth, and be sure to stitch the inner (concave) edge of the stem/vine to the background fabric before the outer (convex) one.

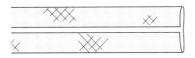 

I f you want your hand-appliquéd shapes to have a little dimension, needleturn the edges and do not press them. For more dimension, needleturned appliqués can also be stuffed. For definition without dimension, use freezer paper to ensure crisply turned edges, then quilt in-the-ditch around the shapes.

Needleturned Appliqué

1. Cut out appliqué shape from fabric, including seam allowance.
2. Pin, glue, or fuse center of shape to background fabric, both right side up, to secure for appliqué.
3. Hand-sew shape in place along seam line, turning under seam allowance with point of needle a bit at a time as you stitch.

◆ *For stuffed appliqué:* With a little bit of the shape's outline still unstitched, insert a small amount of loose fiberfill under the appliqué, then finish stitching.

Freezer Paper Appliqué

1. Cut out one appliqué shape from fabric (with seam allowance) and one from freezer paper (without seam allowance).
2. Center paper shape, coated side up, on wrong side of fabric shape.
3. Fold seam allowance over paper and fuse in place, creasing edges.

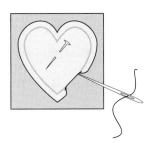

4. Fuse appliqué to background fabric.
5. Hand-sew the appliqué in place, then remove paper through a slit cut in the background fabric.

SLIPSTITCH

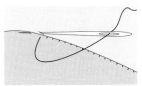

INVISIBLE STITCH

TACKING

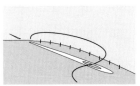

BLANKET STITCH

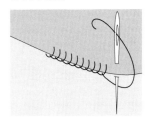

I f you like the look of appliqué but lack the time or patience to do it by hand, machine-appliqué may be for you. You can save time by using heat-sensitive fusibles to stabilize fabric edges for cutting as well as to secure the shapes on the background, eliminating the need for pinning. Machine stitch the appliqués in place with matching, contrasting, or invisible thread.

Basic Machine Appliqué

1. Iron paper-backed fusible web to wrong side of fabric. Mark appliqué shape without seam allowance. Cut out shape along marked lines.
2. Remove paper backing and position shape on background fabric. Iron to fuse shape in place.
3. Machine stitch around appliqué edges.

Machine Satin Stitch

Adjust the stitch width on your sewing machine to between $1/16''$ and $3/16''$, and adjust the stitch length until you achieve a smooth satin (zigzag) stitch. Loosen the upper tension until the top stitches are barely caught on the underside.

Satin stitching can be a little tricky when it comes to corners and curves. At some point you must temporarily stop stitching, with needle down and presser foot up, and pivot the work. Depending on the shapes of your appliqués, you may also have to adjust the stitch width.

INNER/OUTER CORNER

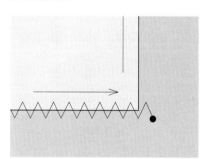

TAPERED POINT/SCALLOP

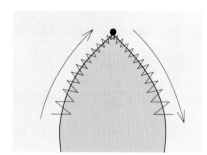

INNER/OUTER CURVE

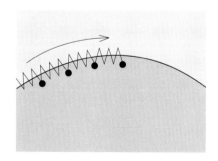

There are many different ways to create guidelines for placement of appliqué, quilting, or embroidery, and some techniques work better for one application than another. Some of the most common marking methods are given below. Use whichever method works best for you and your project.

Marking Methods

If you choose to mark your fabric, be sure to use a nonpermanent marker such as a pencil, pen, or chalk, and always follow the manufacturer's instructions.

TEMPLATES

Make reusable full-size templates from paper, cardboard, or sheet plastic, then trace around them on the fabric.

BACKLIGHTING

Position a full-size paper pattern or tracing behind the fabric, then place in back of them a bright light source and a smooth, clear surface, such as a sunny window, a lightbulb and a sheet of glass, or a lightbox. When the design lines show through on the front of the fabric, trace over them.

DRESSMAKER'S TRACING (CARBON) PAPER

Place dressmaker's carbon between the fabric and a full-size paper pattern or tracing, then go over the design lines wth a dry ball-point pen, stylus, or tracing wheel.

PERFORATED PATTERNS

Draw or trace a full-size pattern on wrapping paper or other sturdy paper. Make perforations on the design lines, using a tracing wheel, unthreaded sewing machine, or sharp pin. Position the paper pattern on the fabric, then go over the perforations with chalk or stamping powder.

Wreath of Flowers Quilt

(pages 6 to 13)

ACTUAL·SIZE PATTERNS

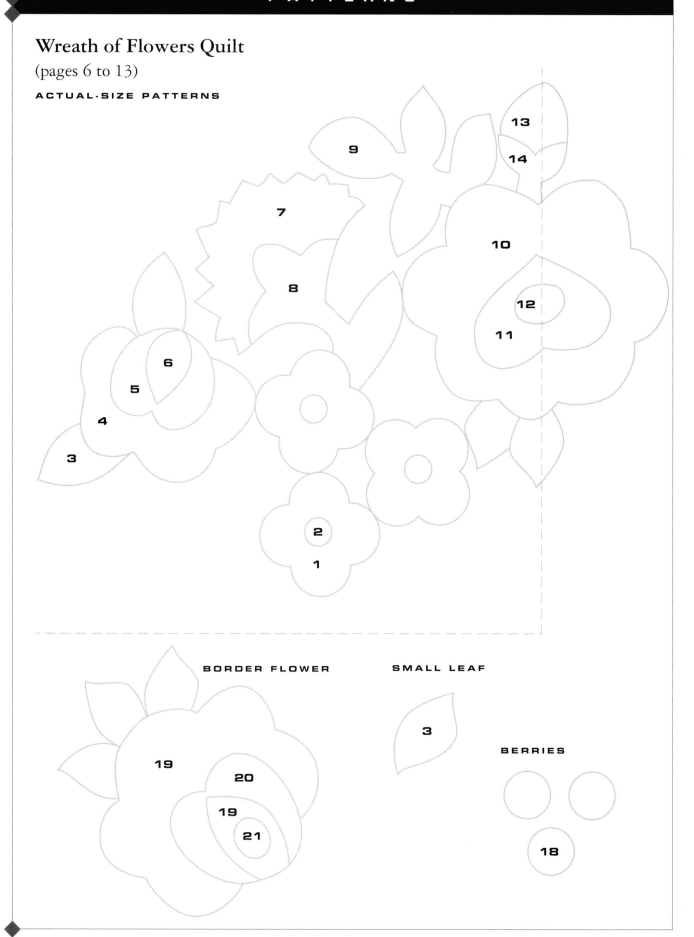

BORDER FLOWER

SMALL LEAF

BERRIES

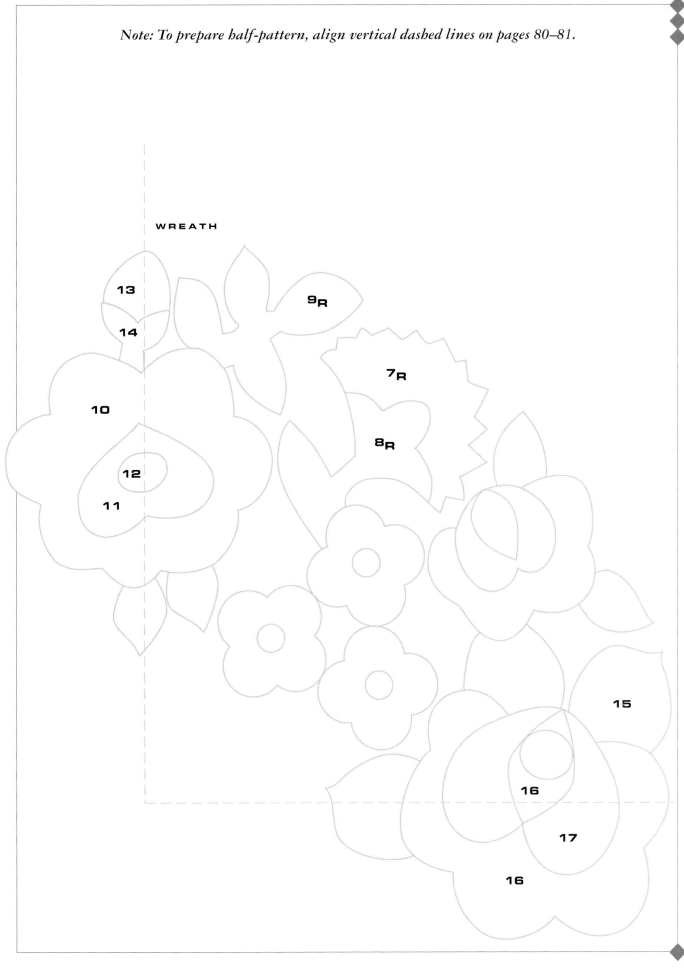

Note: To prepare half-pattern, align vertical dashed lines on pages 80–81.

WREATH

13

14

9R

7R

10

8R

12

11

15

16

17

16

1 SQUARE = 1"
(ENLARGE TO 400%)

ACTUAL-SIZE PATTERNS

Flower and Bud Quilt

(pages 30 to 37)

ACTUAL-SIZE PATTERNS

4

5

3

2

1

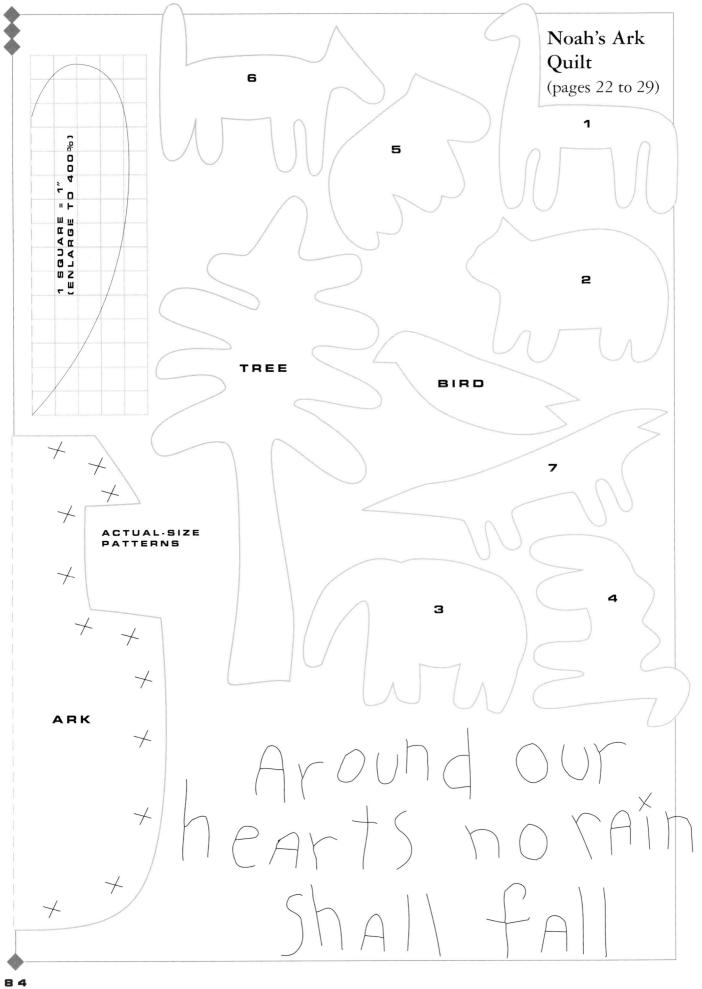

1 SQUARE = 1"
(ENLARGE TO 400%)

6

5

1

2

TREE

BIRD

7

ACTUAL-SIZE
PATTERNS

3

4

ARK

Around our
hearts no rain
shall fall

Rose and Grapes Quilt (pages 38 to 47)

ACTUAL-SIZE PATTERNS

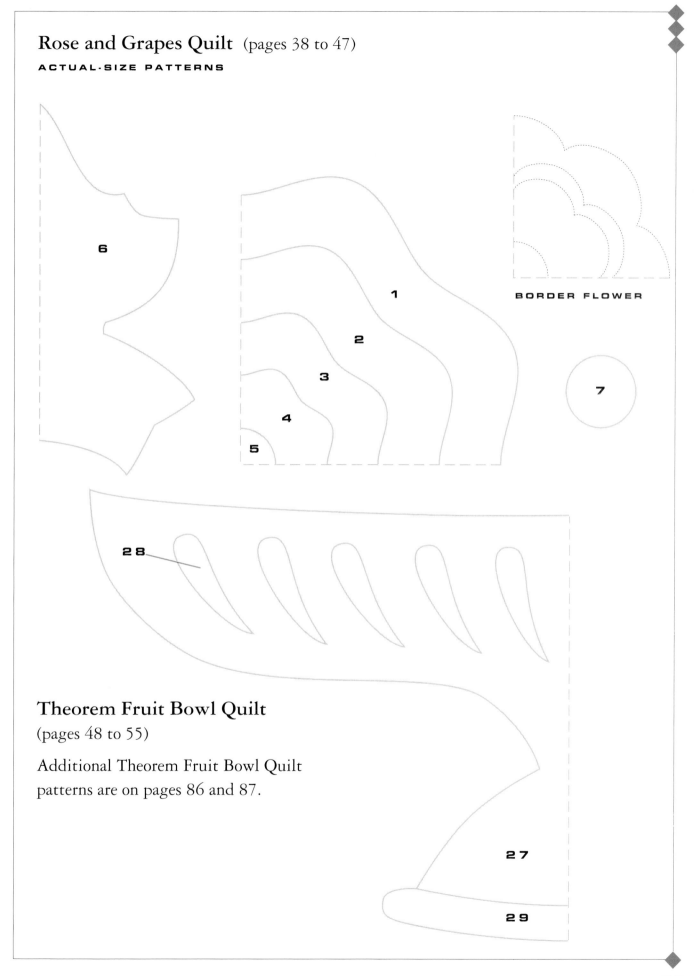

BORDER FLOWER

Theorem Fruit Bowl Quilt

(pages 48 to 55)

Additional Theorem Fruit Bowl Quilt
patterns are on pages 86 and 87.

Theorem Fruit Bowl Quilt

(pages 48 to 55)

ACTUAL-SIZE PATTERN

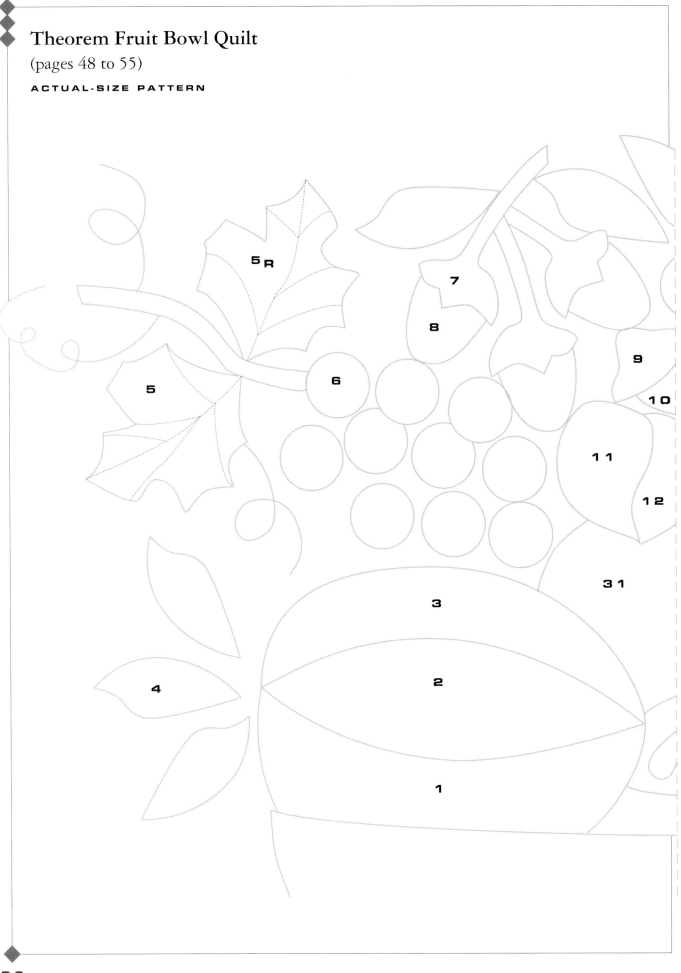

Bears, Bears Everywhere

(pages 66 to 73)

ACTUAL·SIZE PATTERNS

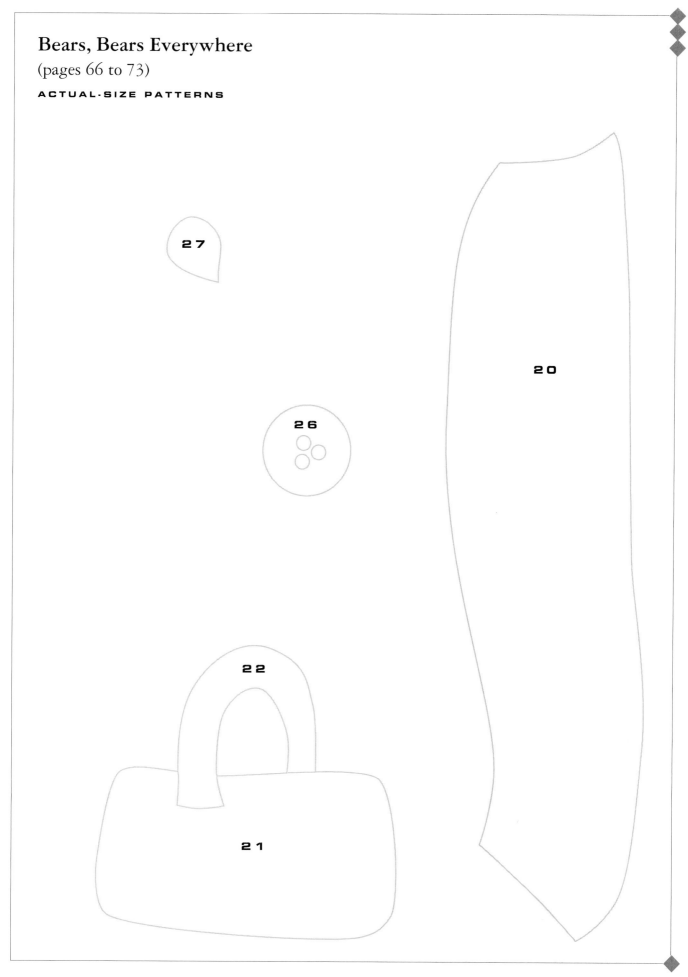

14

36

37

25

34

15

35

16

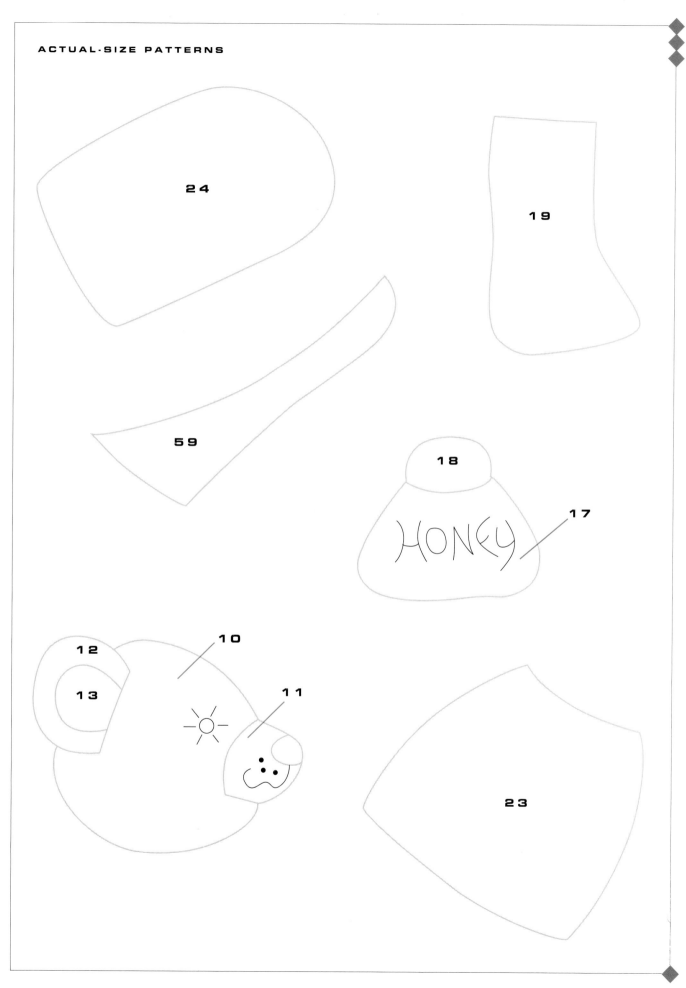

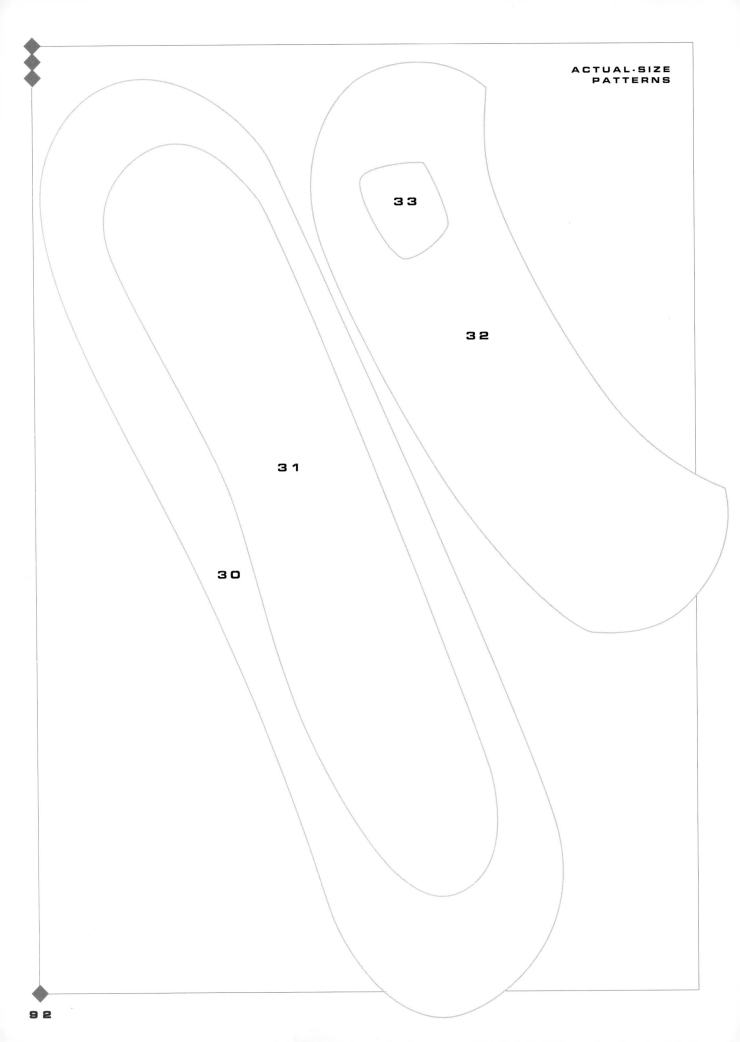

33

32

31

30

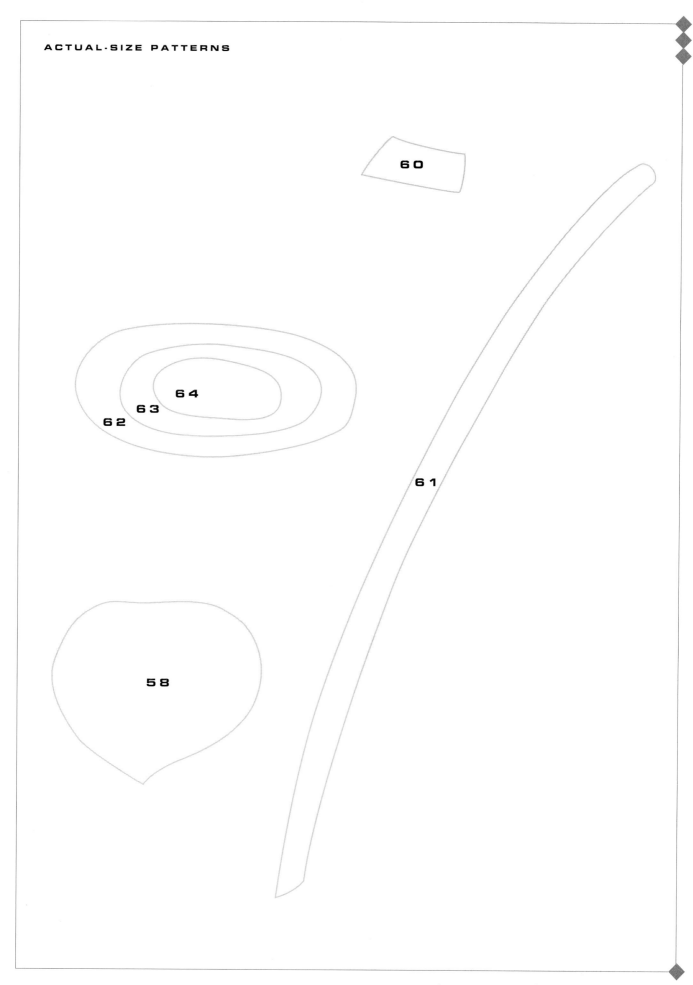

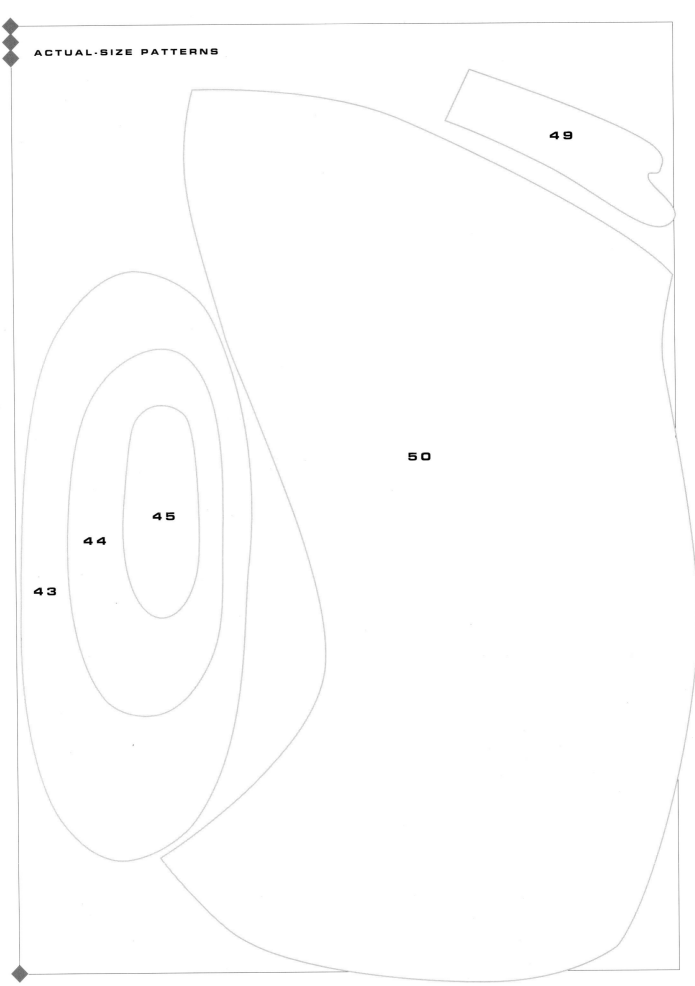

49

50

45

44

43

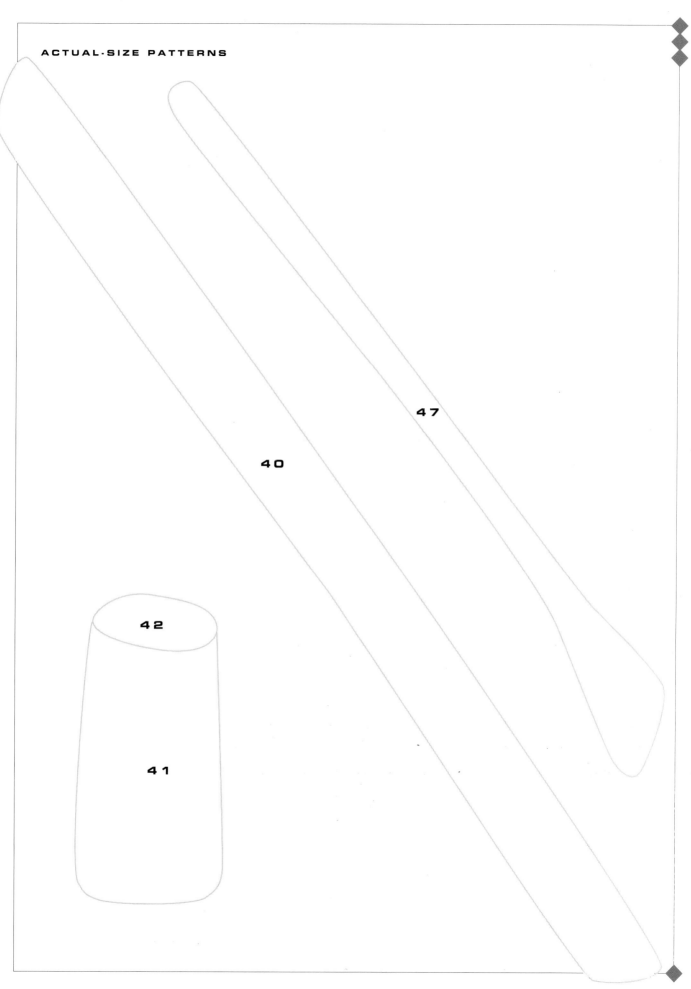

40

47

42

41

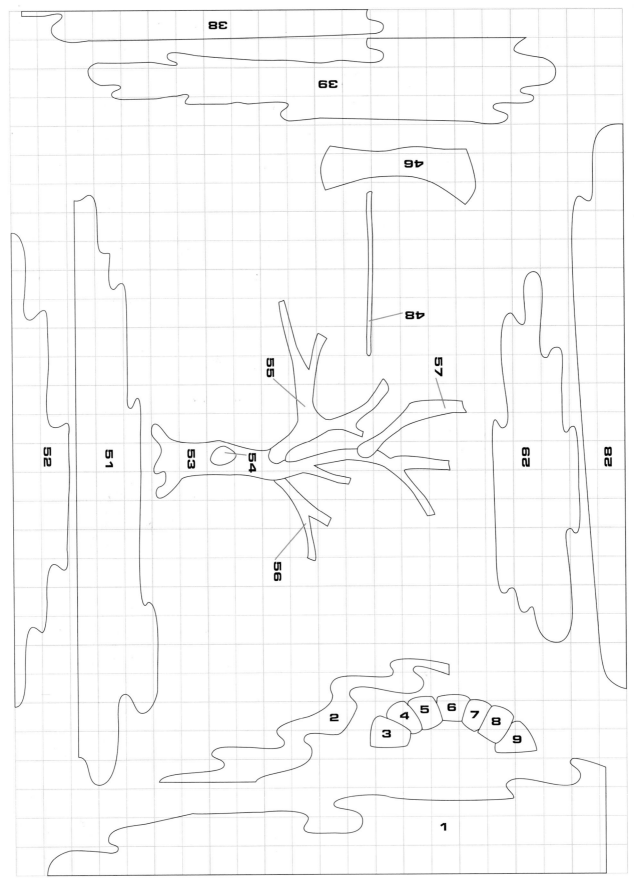